Not Your Ordinary Parenting Book: Newborn Edition

101 Tricks That Take the Guesswork out of Parenting

Happy Parenting!

By: Nicole Coon, Rachel Morrow, and Jennifer Quinn

PHOTO CREDITS

© Ana Vasileva - Fotolia.com

© Lana - Fotolia.com

Special thanks to Robin Belzeski and Krystle Gapol

LIMIT OF LIABILITY/DISCLAIMER OF WARRANTY:

TRADEMARKS

DEDICATION

We dedicate this book to our beautiful children. Without you, our lives would not be nearly as much fun, rewarding, tiring, or exciting. You fill our lives with so much happiness and joy. We love you with all of our hearts, unconditionally. You will always be little babies in our eyes.

TABLE OF CONTENTS

INTRODUCTION

Every parenting book has the same information: suggested shopping lists to prepare for the baby, advice on how to choose a pediatrician, and the American Academy of Pediatrics' recommendations on feeding and sleeping. All of this is great information, but you will find none of it in this book.

Have you ever discovered a little trick to make something much easier? Then you think to yourself, "Man, I wish I figured this out months ago! I could have saved myself so much time and energy!" Well, you are in luck! This book is full of these tricks, discovered by real moms, most of the time after several weeks or months of frustration and trial and error.

Now, every baby and parent is different, of course, but hopefully most of these tricks will help make life a little bit easier for both you and your baby.

Congratulations on your little bundle of joy! Cherish every moment, even the frustrating ones. It really does go by way too fast!

MEET THE MOMS

Rachel Morrow, Jennifer Quinn, Nicole Coon

Jennifer is the mom of Rachel & Nicole – as twins, they were her first two of five children. Now, Rachel is a stay-at-home mom of one and Nicole is a full-time, work-outside-the-home mom of two. Read more about them individually below:

Jennifer

My career of choice is that of Mother. Sure, I have worked jobs to pay the bills, but my passion is nurturing and empowering children to find their voice, their purpose, and their values. I started my Mommy career with two beautiful twin girls. Prior to their birth, I read books on having twins and decided to follow the advice in the books by not giving them "twinsy-sounding" names. I named my daughters Rachel and Nicole (sound familiar?). Two years later, I gave birth to a little tow-headed boy whose name is Travis. After a six year break, I then had a delightful bouncing baby boy named Brian, followed by the baby of the family, another girl, Gabrielle. Now, many years later, not only am I a proud mother of five amazing children, I am a G-MA to three wonderful grandchildren.

Until one becomes a mother, no one can ever tell you what it will feel like to love someone else so deeply and profoundly that you will rejoice when they rejoice, ache when they ache, feel what they feel – even without ever speaking a word.

I will forever be grateful for my children...it started with two, then three, four, five...and blessed beyond all expectations...the family keeps growing through marriages and babies! Miraculously and mysteriously, the capacity to love within my humanness expands exponentially and without effort.

My hope is that as you read this book, you pick up a tip or two which make your parenting journey a little bit easier, and that you might use the time saved by those tips squeezing in one more snuggle or giggle with your child.

Rachel

Growing up, I was the little girl that always wanted to be a mom. In fact, in my third grade talent show, I sang a song called, "When I Grow Up, I Want to Be a Mother*." Seriously. As I grew up, I was lucky enough to meet the man of my dreams at a young age and got married when I was 21 years old. And then I waited. And waited. And waited. And then finally, five years later, my husband and I were ready to start a family! By this point, Nicole, my twin sister, had already had one little boy and was pregnant with her second. I was so excited to finally join her in motherhood! I was so in love with my nephew; I couldn't even imagine what it was going to be like to have one of my own!

In January of 2011, I was blessed with my own little angel from heaven, Madison. She is the sweetest little girl I have ever known, and being a mom has far exceeded my expectations, and they were pretty high expectations! The good part about waiting to start a family is that my husband has a great job so I get to have my dream of being a stay-at-home mom come true! I have learned so many little tricks from my mom and my sister to make taking care of Madison so much easier, and I have even discovered some new tricks of my own. I am so excited to get to share these tricks with you, so you can spend less time with the trial-and-error process and more time enjoying your little angel!

*words and lyrics by Geneen Brady

Nicole

I am the type of mother that loves the family bed, and my kids live a pretty relaxed life with minimal routines. I was fortunate enough to have my life go according to plan when I got pregnant after being married for a year-and-a-half. I welcomed my little monkey, Treydon, into the world in September of 2008. Almost two years later, my little man, Tyler, was born. Both of my boys are very "chill" as my husband would say, and that is something that we take great pride in. They are very happy boys, with huge smiles that can make anyone's day. I am very lucky to be their mother.

While growing up, I wasn't really into babies: as my twin sister, Rachel, was rocking her baby doll and singing "When I Grow Up, I Want to Be a Mother" in our third grade talent show, I was singing and dancing to "Surfin' U.S.A." with my best friend. My own mom actually told me (after I became a mom) that she was a little nervous for me to be a mom, because growing up she had never seen the nurturing side of me. But luckily, once I heard my little boy's first cry, my world was turned upside down and I would never be the same. Mothering instantly became second nature to me, I even surprised myself! Parenting is definitely a unique journey that each mom has to discover on her own.

I am a work-outside-the-home mom, and for the past three-and-a-half years I have been the primary provider for my family, while my husband has embraced the stay-at-home dad role. This was never part of our original plan, but what is in life? Every day is a struggle to juggle the demands of work with the joys of being a mother, but I feel like I have done a pretty decent job so far. Since babies don't come with instruction manuals, I spent many hours figuring out what made my boys tick. It was fun for me when Rachel had her little baby girl, because I was able to share small tidbits of information with her that I had learned along the way! I hope that by sharing these tips and tricks with you I will save you: money – from buying the wrong type of baby product; time – from having to try multiple methods to find one that works; and many sleepless nights (and anything to get some more sleep is worth a shot). Here's to all the parents in the world – the most important job that offers no training and previous experience doesn't matter!

Nicole with her boys and Rachel with her girl

SLEEP

From the very beginning, have noise on when putting your baby to sleep.

The idea is that she will be used to the noise so it will not wake her up. I have done this from the very beginning, but Madison is naturally a very light sleeper, so I still have to be cautious. The blow dryer or vacuum will not wake her up, but if I talk, her little eyes pop open. She doesn't want to miss a thing.

I did this with Tyler from the beginning as well, and now whenever it's time to go to bed, I just turn on the noise maker and, viola, he falls quickly asleep. Also, invest in a portable noise maker for trips (smiles).

Also, from the beginning, purposely have the baby fall asleep in different locations to keep her from getting attached to only one place for sleep.

AH! SHOOT!! Mom... where was this tip for me?? I just spent a week long vacation – I mean a week long, sleepless vacation with my little man because he won't sleep anywhere but his crib!

Remember when I was helping you get him settled in the crib and I suggested putting him to sleep in the pack 'n play in a different room for naps?

Active listening has never been something I've been good at (smiles).

Use a HALO® SleepSack to swaddle – it's a miracle worker!!

Seriously, it is so easy to use! You don't even need to worry about how to swaddle with a blanket like they do at the hospital.

It is the best brand, for sure! I tried several! But make sure to have the Velcro fastened when you wash it, otherwise it will not last very long.

I love this product. I didn't have them when I was raising babies. My mom had taught me how to bundle the baby tightly with a receiving blanket (which is still an option). The HALO® sleep sack is infinitely easier, more effective, and safer. Definitely worth the investment.

The swaddle needs to be really tight, tighter than you think.

If it is not tight enough, you may think your baby does not like being swaddled. That happened to me. Once I got it tight enough, Madison slept very well. I'm so thankful I stuck with the swaddle! If your baby can move her arms at all, it is too loose.

Also, if it's not tight enough, your little monkey will wiggle his arms out in no time, thus defeating the purpose of the swaddle in the first place.

The reason for swaddling is two-fold. Primarily, it keeps your baby feeling safe, like when he was in the womb. It is very soothing for a newborn to be swaddled tightly. Another reason for swaddling your baby is to keep him from hitting himself in the head with his flailing arms, which he has no control over. To him, if his arm hits him in the face or head, he is alarmed as if it was a foreign object coming out of nowhere!

Only swaddle at night so your baby associates it with long sleep.

 I did this, and it works! Madison was sleeping up to 12 hours straight at two months old!

I did this starting with my second and it worked like a charm as well! Nothing is more relieving than the first night your baby sleeps more than three hours at a time.

Again, the swaddling is so comforting to the baby that he will sleep longer while he is swaddled, so this prevents long naps during the day and teaches him about day and night sleep cycles.

Keep your newborn up for a minimum of two hours before putting him to sleep for the night, even if he is a bit grumpy. This will ensure you a better night's sleep.

I actually learned this from Nicole while we were writing this book. Thank you, Nicole! It really does work!

I wonder where Nicole learned this trick from.

Was it from you? (smiles) Sometimes you don't remember where you hear it from.

Sleep-deprivation as a new mommy is my guess! This particular trick is a challenge because it is so difficult to keep a fussy baby awake. Your dad and I used to spend two hours entertaining, playing, singing, and bouncing the two of you each evening. Of course, the real trick is getting Mom and Dad to go to bed at the same time the baby does.

If your baby falls asleep in your arms, hold her for 10 minutes before putting her down.

 This one was a lifesaver for me! Before I did this, Madison would always wake up right when I would put her down. She still wakes up sometimes after I wait the 10 minutes, but not nearly as much as before I started doing this.

Every baby is different, too. With my second, he required 20 minutes before being put down or he would wake up and want to play.

The tell-tale sign your little one has fallen asleep is when she lets out the big sigh, followed by full-body relaxation. If using a binky, the binky will fall out and she won't let you put it back in. That's how you know for sure that she will stay asleep if you lay her down.

If your baby wakes up in the middle of the night screaming, try burping him.

It seems that about 80% of the time my boys just had a big burp they couldn't get out. This happened to me just last night, only I forgot my own tip and spent too long trying to figure out what was wrong before he burped, and then spit up all over me (see tip on page 65 about moving baby horizontal after they burp, which I also forgot). Ha-ha!!

This is true more than you might realize! I didn't start testing for burps until we were writing this book…and what do you know, more times than not there was a big burp waiting to come out!

Many newborns need an incline to sleep; the Fisher Price Newborn Rock 'n Play™ Sleeper works great for those babies.

Great is an understatement! The only way I could get Madison to sleep was by holding her, until I got this! Plus you can put it right next to your bed, and just reach down and rock it when your baby starts fussing.

This was not around when I had my first, and I had to resort to having him sleep in my bed with one of those co-sleepers that had an incline (which have since been recalled) because he had acid reflux. It took me until he was two-and-a-half to get him to sleep in his own bed because we started out this way. I then discovered this product with my second baby. He didn't sleep in my bed for even one night, which is good, since my toddler was still in it at the time! It is also great because it is very portable and easy to travel with!! Especially easy to travel up to see G-MA, which she appreciates!

Check with your pediatrician to see if she recommends a head cradle pillow to use in the Rock 'n Play to prevent flat head.

Invest in a video sleep monitor; the peace of mind is worth every penny.

I am one of those moms that wake up every hour to make sure my baby is still breathing. Having the video monitor made it so I could leave the room and not have to risk waking Madison up to check on her.

Ha-ha. I just keep the kiddos in my room, built in "baby monitor".

I never had any kind of monitor, but it certainly is fun to see pictures that Rachel sends of the monitor screen showing Madison sleeping! Rachel, you really should insert the picture of her sleeping straight up in the crib that we would have never known about without the monitor. I love that picture! (see page 40)

Leave one of your worn shirts near your baby (NOT IN THE CRIB) when she is sleeping in another room. This leaves your scent behind and can give your baby a sense of security.

Another lifesaver! This trick allowed me to finally shower while Madison was taking a nap.

I never tried this one, but Tyler became very attached to a "lovey" that he cannot sleep without! So that is another idea to give your little one an added sense of security.

Yes! And if you do use a "lovey", you should wear it around in your shirt for a day or two so that it absorbs your smell. It sounds weird, but it works.

When your baby goes from sleeping well to waking up more frequently throughout the night, it could be a sign his tummy is growing and you need to increase how much food you give him before bed.

If you are breastfeeding, you can do this by feeding one hour before bedtime, and again right before you put him down. For Madison, this happened at four months. Nothing is wrong with your baby, and you didn't do anything wrong to make him start waking up more, he is just growing. If the waking up continues, it may be time to start solids.

G-MA actually discovered this one while she was watching my boys while my husband and I were out of town. She upgraded his bottle at bedtime from 4 oz. to 8 oz. and he went from waking up twice per night to sleeping from 9:30 PM to 7:00 AM straight through! Thanks G-MA!!

You're welcome! This is why it is very, very, very important to have G-MA uber involved in baby raising. Sometimes parents are just too busy surviving to notice these little things. Just sayin'…

As your baby gets a little older and can grasp things, sprinkle pacifiers around the crib so that in the middle of the night he can find one no matter where he is.

If you followed my advice and got the video monitor, it is very entertaining to watch your baby grab the pacifiers in her sleep. I could not believe how talented she was!

This is a tip from G-MA! I used it on Trey and it worked like a charm! But be forewarned...you will be finding binkies hidden under your crib for months to come.

If I'm not mistaken, your Dad thought of this trick, and it works so well! It turned into a great little ritual at bedtime. A binky in the mouth, one for each hand, and a few sprinkled around the head was sure to bring giggles from the baby!

The ideal window of opportunity to get your baby to sleep independently is before six months. At that time, he enters the "attachment stage."

I was told this by our pediatrician at my son's seven-month check-up...bummer – too late! So, I thought I would share it with you all so you could take advantage of the knowledge before it is too late!

Thank you for this tip, Nicole! I was able to start getting Madison to break out of her attachment stage before it was too late.

If you are trying to encourage your baby to sleep through the night, when she wakes up during the night, turn on as few lights as needed to meet her needs. Don't talk to her or make it "fun". Simply change her diaper quietly, feed her quietly, and then gently put her back to sleep.

It is hard not to talk to her, but well worth it. I have done this since day one, and every time Madison wakes up at night, she eats and goes right back to sleep. I hold her for 10 minutes (see page 19), and then we are both right back in bed.

You can't make it a party, or they will want to wake up and join the fun! But it's so hard not to make them smile or give them a little tickle.

This one is so hard because warm little babies are so yummy in the middle of the night when it's all quiet. But, long term it is worth it. Besides, once baby is back asleep, you can always sneak in and hold her. The idea is to teach the baby that the middle of the night is not a fun time to play.

As your baby gets older and you and your doctor are certain she is getting enough food during the daytime, try giving her only water when she wakes up in the middle of the night. Soon she will learn that waking up at night isn't really worth it.

So true. I used to offer water in the bottle if the baby woke up. This taught the baby that waking up at night was not as much fun as it is during the day time. Please check with your pediatrician on which age is appropriate to do this and what type of water is best for your area.

Or just try to get your baby back to sleep without anything. If I just pat Madison's back and sing to her, she will go back to sleep most of the time. I still have the bottle ready to go, just in case it doesn't work, but usually I don't need it.

DIAPERING

Get all of your supplies ready BEFORE you lay your baby down to diaper – even pull out the wipes first.

This sounds so simple, doesn't it? I can't tell you how many times I have been surprised at what I found in the diaper while changing it when I was only expecting a wet diaper. By then, it is a little too late to be prepared. And these little babies are strong! Their legs want to flail all over the place, making an even bigger mess.

Pulling out the wipes is very important! I found that the wipes tend to stick together when you are pulling them out of the tub, and if you don't do it ahead of time, it can really slow down your diaper changing. I always pull out more than I think I will need. I can always shove the unused ones back in the box.

And if you don't do it beforehand, you may get some pee on you while you are trying to get the wipes out...just sayin'. Not that it's ever happened to me before (smiles).

Place the new diaper under the baby's bum before removing the old one – this way, if your baby decides to "surprise" you with something mid-change you are prepared.

Learned this one from a more "experienced" mom when I had my first! I cannot count the times it has saved me from a huge poopy mess.

This also decreases your diaper changing time a lot! Especially helpful when you are in a public bathroom!

Boys – Point the penis down before closing up the diaper, so pee does not leak out the top.

Learned this one the hard way! After about a week-and-a-half of my first boy leaking through every single night, I finally discovered the trick (smiles)!

Yes! And while changing a baby boy, hold the clean diaper above the penis in case he decides to pee while you are changing him.

Vaseline® works just as good as any diaper rash cream and is much cheaper!

It really does, and if you haven't looked at diaper creams, they are quite expensive. Unfortunately, I did not realize that Vaseline® works just as good until my second boy was about two months old and I had misplaced my expensive diaper rash cream, so I used it out of desperation, only to find out I had been wasting my money for two years!

Another great tip I learned from writing this book together! Love it!

Bag Balm® works better than Vaseline® and is almost as cheap! (Find it in a drug store – not with baby stuff – it is sold in a green square tin – originally used for cows' udders!)

This is my favorite diaper rash product. Use a tiny bit after each changing and you likely won't have any sores, rashes, redness, or bleeding. It acts as a barrier between your baby's skin and the mess.

I remember that green square tin from when we were little!

Do you also remember your youngest brother "painting" your baby sister with the Bag Balm®? Oy – what a mess!

All diapers have a built-in elastic barrier around the crotch area; make sure to pull it out around your baby's bum after putting the diaper on.

HA-HA!! This is definitely a new mom mistake... I think it took my husband and me two weeks of blowouts to discover the actual way to put on a diaper. We both felt pretty stupid, but nobody had ever shown us before.

Luckily, thanks to Nicole, I did not have to learn the hard way with this one.

Buy disposable changing pads to cover your regular changing pad; it makes blowouts way easier to clean up. Only change it out if it gets dirty, that way it is very affordable.

These make cleaning blowouts up at home so much easier! They are also great to pack in the diaper bag for those germ-covered public changing stations.

Wish I would have had this tip! I had to wash my cover almost every day!

Invest in a diaper pail. Well worth it!

And don't forget the baking soda disks to go in it!

I actually prefer keeping plastic grocery bags or zipper baggies handy, and then take them out to the garbage. Something about a pail full of soiled diapers makes me a little ill.

They all end up in the same place...I love my diaper pail!

Diaper pails are a must-have if you have a two-story home for sure! Who wants to walk downstairs with a poopy diaper to take it to the trash everytime? If you live on a one-level house, they are still very beneficial, but not as much of a neccessity.

Maybe we can compromise and use individual bags to wrap the diapers in before placing the soiled diapers in the diaper pail? Baking soda disks can only absorb so much odor.

If you notice that your baby is having more blowouts than usual, it is time to move up a diaper size.

It always took me too long with each diaper size to realize this. Madison always looked like she was wearing too big of diapers, but the bigger the diaper, the more room for the poop to go before it leaks out. She was wearing size 3 at 13 pounds.

They go through the first four sizes super fast, typically all within the first year... so don't stock pile too much of sizes newborn – 3. Size 4, however, my boys wore for a very long time, like two years.

As your baby gets older and starts to eat more before bed, he will soak through his diapers at night. If he is big enough for a size 3 diaper, buy the overnight diapers – well worth the money! If your baby is too small still (they only make overnights starting in size 3), put on a size 2 and layer it with a size 3.

 Learned this one after about two months of having to wake up my one year old in the middle of the night just so that he wouldn't wake up soaked in his own pee. I never even knew overnight diapers existed! Now, my second boy started soaking through them at a much younger age, so he did not fit into a size 3 yet, hence the layering technique I discovered, that works just as well. Except when you combine this with the layering pajamas trick (see page 86) you get a little dough boy looking baby. HA-HA – so cute!

Madison asleep in her crib, captured
by the video monitor
(see page 22)

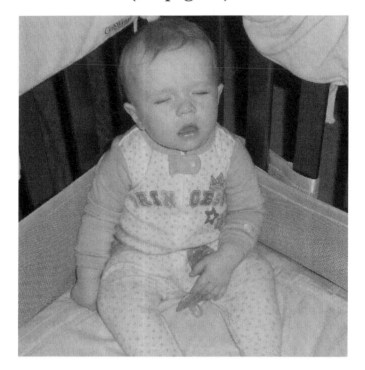

BREASTFEEDING

It doesn't have to hurt in the beginning. In fact, if it does hurt, you probably do not have the correct latch.

You know you have the correct latch if your baby's lower lip is sticking out over your breast, not tucked under. At the beginning, I had my husband manually pull Madison's lower lip out if it was tucked under. My hands were busy trying to figure out how to hold her properly. After a week or two, she got it right every time.

The time invested in working with a lactation specialist in the hospital or in your community is well worth it. Breastfeeding is an art and a skill. You don't have to learn it all on your own. Contact your local Le Leche League chapter, or ask at the OB ward in the hospital. If you haven't had your baby yet, now is a good time to start learning!

That is so true; to start learning before the baby is born. I actually read the chapter on breastfeeding in my parenting book several times so that I had it all memorized. I even acted out the movements it described with my hands so I would easily be able to remember the technique. It came in very handy when my daughter was born.

If you make sure you have the correct latch every time, and put lanolin on afterwards for the first month, you will not get the bleeding and cracking everyone talks about.

 I was so afraid to breastfeed after hearing so many horror stories. I put the lanolin on after every feeding, whether it hurt or not, for the first month, and I never had any bleeding or cracking.

 I wish someone would have told me this! I was the mom who had the cracked, bleeding nipples for the first month of Treydon's life. Rachel probably learned from my mistakes (smiles).

I'm pretty sure I told you this. I'm just saying.

Sometimes new moms are stubborn (smiles).

Yes, I did learn from your mistakes. That's the benefit of having my baby second, I suppose (smiles).

If you have the luxury of time and privacy, airing out your breast after nursing is a great way to prevent problems, too. Mother's milk has a natural component to prevent drying.

Change your hand, thumb, and wrist position frequently. This will help prevent tendinitis.

This happened to me! It is so painful to feed and hold your baby with tendinitis! And it took two months of not using my thumb for it to heal. I wish I could go back in time and follow this trick!

Yes! Also change sides and angles of the baby. This will help with both the latching-on-the-nipple tenderness and your own body aches. New moms don't realize that when they are nursing they can be very tense. So, in addition to trying to relax more while breastfeeding, make sure you change positions frequently.

Pump bottles for your partner to help you feed and give you a break (especially in the middle of the night).

This was a lifesaver for me, especially when I went back to work. It was great to be able to have a helping hand in the middle of the night. Daddy enjoyed the time too.

I never had the patience for pumping, but if you do, more power to you! It will give you a nice break!

And just know that it will take a couple of days of pumping for your body to begin producing more milk, so don't get discouraged. It also helps if you do it at around the same time everyday so your body can have the milk ready.

Invest in a breastfeeding pillow! It is well worth it, and will save your arm muscles.

My favorite is the Boppy®! Your arms will thank you! I actually have two, one in the bedroom for nighttime feedings and one in the living room for day feedings.

And it is worth it to buy a new one rather than get a hand me down. It also works great for travel! You can also use it to prop up your baby when he is beginning to learn to sit.

The Boppy® is much easier than using a lot of pillows, but a lot of pillows will work too.

Everyone says if you breastfeed, the weight will drop right off. In reality, breastfeeding only helps with weight loss after three months. Most women hit a plateau between one and three months postpartum.

 I was getting so frustrated because I was breastfeeding exclusively and kept waiting for the weight to fall off like everyone said it would. Once I hit the three-month mark, bam! I consistently lost a pound a week (I did exercise and watch what I ate).

I never lost any weight until about month four with both of my boys, but I did not know this tip, so I spent too much time beating myself up over not losing the weight.

And some of us take about 16+ years to lose the weight. Oh, wait. We are talking about post-partum weight? Disregard.

G-MA with her grandkids

BOTTLE FEEDING

Cereal nipples exist!! Look up "Tri-Cut Nipple." To make a consistency that your baby can suck through the bottle, mix 1 tsp. of rice cereal per 2 oz. of formula/breast milk. Don't use until your baby is a minimum of four months old.

Can anyone say LIFESAVER? This also fills up his tummy more so he sleeps better. I only use when I am putting my little man to sleep.

Consider storing the cereal nipples in a separate place than the milk nipples. Nothing good can come from adding the wrong one to a bottle, right, Nicole? Nicole's little guy was given the wrong nipple with a cereal bottle and the babysitter couldn't figure out why he wasn't eating all day. Oh my goodness! Poor guy!

When your baby starts to get frustrated when eating, that means it's time to switch to the fast-flow nipple.

Learned this when one of my sister-in-laws was watching my boys for me, and she informed me that I needed to switch nipples. Some things you just don't think of on your own – hence this book being compiled.

There are also variable flow nipples, so you can change the flow based on which way the bottle is turned. You can use these as your baby grows.

When going to bed, place pre-measured formula in a clean bottle on your nightstand with a bottle of water.

Doing this makes nighttime feedings a breeze and reduces middle of the night thinking (smiles). I always struggled with measuring formula half asleep.

They actually make water bottles that are exactly 8 oz., so you can even pour the water in without seeing how much it is. Not exactly cost effective, but very handy for the middle of the night.

Put Dawn® Direct Foam by your sink. It makes cleaning a bottle quick and easy.

 Best invention ever! It saves so much time since you don't have to fill up the sink with water and add the regular dish soap just to clean one bottle. I even take a bottle of Dawn® with me when traveling – that's how much I love it!

It is very convenient, that's for sure! I am a fan!

I have inherited many bottles of Dawn® foaming soap from Nicole after a visit. Score!

Nicole and her boys

SOLID FOODS

Include your baby in your family meals before she is ready for solid foods, this way she can SEE how you eat and can mimic this behavior when the time comes for her to eat.

This is important for the baby's development. Babies learn by imitation. While you are putting food in your mouth, chewing, and swallowing, your baby is watching and trying to figure it out long before she is ready to start eating herself. If she is never with you while you are eating until you want her to eat, she will not know what to do.

I made this mistake with Tyler. We always ate on a different schedule than he did and he never saw us eat. When I started trying to feed him food he had no clue what to do with it! That is until G-MA came to the rescue and had to teach him how to swallow!

Mix rice cereal with baby food – it's a great combination of texture and taste that your baby may enjoy.

Tyler wouldn't eat rice cereal. He also wouldn't eat baby food. But when I mixed the two together, he ate like a champ!

I also think the cereal acts as a thickener. Most baby foods are too watery once the baby has the concept of swallowing mastered. Using cereal can make it the right consistency for your baby.

I tried this and Madison will not eat it. She loves each individually, but not together. Every baby truly is different!

If your baby does not like a particular food, try experimenting with different temperatures.

 Madison hated carrots and peas at room temperature, but when I refrigerate them first, she eats them right up! You can also try heating up the foods.

And my boys wouldn't eat any baby food once it was refrigerated. They liked it a room temperature.

Keep a bottle of Wet Ones® next to the high chair (they make some that are baby safe). This makes it much quicker and easier to clean your little one after feeding.

 These are great because then you can just throw them away and you don't have to worry about smelly wash clothes, lots of laundry, or the germs that a washcloth can hold.

I use alcohol-free baby wipes for this, the sensitive ones.

Give your baby a spoon to hold while you feed her to occupy her hands.

She will love feeling like she is helping, plus she will be more ready to feed herself when the time comes.

This is a good tip! I wish I would have had that idea with my little ones. Instead it was a constant battle of getting the spoon into his mouth before his hand hit it and splattered it all over the place.

Mum-Mum® rice crackers are a good first finger food for your baby. They can keep him happy while you are preparing his food, or grabbing a bite for yourself!

And they dissolve very easily! I used these before any other solid foods. They also keep him happy while strolling at the mall!

These dissolve so fast, if you are feeding your baby solids, you can feed her these! Very handy!

Rachel and Madison (note the brace for the
tendinitis, see page 44)

SPIT-UP

Burp your baby mid-way through a feeding to reduce spit-up.

At first, your baby will be upset that you stopped him from eating, but with time, he will learn that there is more food to come.

Also burp before feeding if he has been crying. Crying brings in a lot of unwanted air.

When you hear your baby burp, immediately lay him horizontal. Many times spit-up will follow.

I had to change my shirt so many times a day until I learned this trick!

This is a very handy tip to know right off the bat! You will save yourself a lot of clean-up!

Make sure to lie your baby on his side or tummy to reduce chances of choking, just in case he is about to spit up.

After your baby eats, or when you hear your baby burp, do not hold her over your head to see how cute she is. EWWWW....spit up in the mouth.

It only takes one time to learn this trick. I am simply trying to save you that one time experience.

Very true. My one time was with my little brother. Luckily, I learned this lesson early.

HA-HA! Growing up I heard the story of Rachel and our little brother many times! I remember being jealous because she got a soda after it happened, and we never got soda growing up. Now that I am older, I realize that soda was a horrible consolation prize. Needless to say, I never made this mistake either, the story was on the forefront of my mind.

Don't sit your baby up until 30 minutes after eating – keep him lying down. This will greatly reduce the spit-up.

I wish I would have known this during those first few months! It would have saved me so much time spent cleaning up spit-up.

This is a great tip if you have a baby that spits up all the time! Trey had acid reflux, so keeping him lying down was the only way that he could actually keep his meal down.

To prevent a rash in your baby's neck rolls from too much drool, put baby powder in the creases.

 I put it on my arm first and then used my finger to apply it in the creases to prevent Madison from inhaling the powder.

Regular kitchen cornstarch works well for this (or in diapering, as well) because cornstarch has an absorbency quality.

This is a great idea!! The boys always got a rash in their necks. How often do you do it?

I just do it after every bath, so a few times a week.

Baby wipes work great to clean spit-up out of your clothes and the carpet.

I never have to change my shirt anymore. I just wipe the spit-up with the baby wipe, and as soon as my shirt (or pants) dries, it is as good as new! Also, sensitive wipes work better for this because they do not leave behind any white lint from the wipe.

And much more cost efficient than any stain remover pads! Plus, you always have a wipe on you if your baby is near!

If you notice your baby spitting up the most when she is in the sitting position, you may be tightening the diaper waistband too tightly.

It took me too long to figure this out. Madison was always spitting up when I would hold her sitting up on my waist, when she was in her walker, and other various positions where she was "sitting", but rarely any other times. I figured something had to be pushing on her stomach. So I tried fastening her diaper much looser than I had been. Voila! She went from spitting up about 10 times per day to only one or two.

HA-HA! I've never heard this before. Funny what things you don't realize you are doing as a new mom.

TEETHING

When you notice a lot of drool coming out of your baby's mouth, more than usual, that is one of the first signs that teething has begun.

So load up on the Baby Orajel®, Tylenol®, and start napping whenever possible... you have some long nights ahead of you (smiles).

With Madison, the first sign of teething is not sleeping very well. She always has a lot of drool. Also, I prefer baby ibuprofen instead of acetaminophen because it lasts eight hours instead of four.

Use the Baby Orajel® Medicated Toothache Swabs. They make it much easier to apply the medicine to your crying baby's gums than having to rub the Orajel® on your fingertip and then try to maneuver it in your baby's mouth.

Although it is never an easy feat to get any teething medicine into a little baby's mouth, these make it significantly easier.

So true, Madison would always try to eat my finger when I would put the Orajel® on it, but for some reason, she opens her mouth right up for the swab.

Keep a few of your baby's teething toys in the fridge at all times so you will always have one ready to go when you need it.

This is a lifesaver for when those teeth suddenly show up! I keep Madison's in a plastic baggie so they don't absorb anything from the food in the fridge. I don't know if that could really happen, but hey, it's better safe than sorry.

Back in the "old days" we used to keep clean, wet, washcloths in the refrigerator to give to the baby to chew on when teething. The texture of the washcloth was soothing, in addition to being cold.

Keep up on where your baby's growth is in relation to medicine dosing charts.

When I watched Trey & Ty, Nicole left instructions on how much Tylenol® to give Ty for teething. It didn't seem like enough, so I looked it up. It turns out that time had flown by so fast that Ty needed three or four times as much as Nicole said to give him. He was still receiving the newborn dosage (another reason it is very, very, very important to have G-MA uber involved).

It is very easy for time to slip away, that's for sure! An easy way to find out your baby's current weight (so that you can get an accurate dose) is to weigh yourself first, and then weigh yourself again while holding your baby. Then you can look up dosing charts online, or make a quick call to your pediatrician.

Trey and Ty showing their Bronco pride!

GAS

A few drops of water do the same thing as gas medicine.

I use a medicine syringe for this. A little goes a long way. I only give Madison 2 mL or so.

Really?? Who would've thunk!? I didn't do this with either boy...but I sure forked over quite a bit of money for some gas medicine at the store.

Make your baby do the "bicycle" with her legs to help relieve gas.

This also works as a preventative measure. Plus, your baby will probably think you are playing with her!

Works great to help relieve adult gas too! Ha-ha, just kidding. My husband actually discovered this one for us – and always made a fun game out of it. The boys were just laughing away as they were farting up a storm. Pretty humorous – get the video camera out.

Nicole, I've heard it said that behind every joke is an element of truth. *wink*

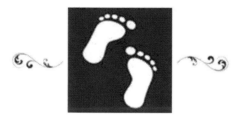

If formula feeding, Gentlease® formula works miracles on gas.

This was the third formula I tried. I have two half-full containers of formula just sitting at my house that I will never use. Now you can save fifty bucks and buy this one the first time around (smiles).

I never had to use formula, but I imagine this would be very helpful!

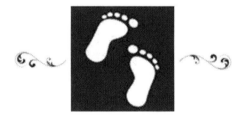

CLOTHING

Only invest in a few "cute" outfits in each size for the first year. The majority of the time your baby will be at home, and body suits (Onesies®)/sleepers are perfectly sufficient (especially the newborn size – they rarely leave home).

You should have seen the outfits I put Madison in to go to the doctor. Hey, somebody had to see her cute clothes!

I got so many cute outfits with my first boy. I wanted to save the cute ones for an outing or get-together, but then he grew out of the size and he only got to wear each cute outfit once or twice, if even at all. I quickly learned you do not need that many "going out" outfits, unless of course, you go out all the time!

Newborn and 0-3 months are two different sizes. Newborn is smaller.

 I thought I had so many clothes to start out with, but every time I would put an outfit on, it was too big. It turns out I only had three actual newborn outfits, oops!

I made the opposite mistake: I had all size newborn and very few size 0-3 months. So Trey grew out of newborn size very fast, but size 3-6 months were still too big for him. Same rule applies for diapers – newborn and size 1 are also different.

Get Carter's® Bubble Socks, they stay on much better than any other kind.

This is a tip from G-MA that she learned while raising her kids! Thanks for sharing! These socks kept my boys' feet warm for many a days!

Yes they do! I put the three-month size on Madison as a newborn and they still stayed on!

Yes, these are the only style of booties that stay on to keep the little feet warm all night. I used to put them on under the sleeper for extra warmth.

You really can have too many Onesies® and sleepers.

Although only one of us three moms has reached that point (of having too many Onesies®; you know who you are). Plan on about 10-15 Onesies® and 10-12 sleepers in each size, unless you are super woman and do laundry all of the time, like only one of us three moms (you know who YOU are).

If your baby is anything like mine, you will have to do laundry several times a week, unless you want poop clothes sitting around. If you wait to wash the poop clothes, they may stain.

HA-HA – I would rather buy more Onesies® than do laundry all the time! Also, I throw away Onesies® that are full of poop.

If your baby likes to sleep really warmly, as he gets older and is too old for swaddling, try layering a thick blanket sleeper, over a thin regular sleeper, over a Onesie®. When your baby wakes up in the morning, you can remove the blanket sleeper, and if it didn't get soiled, you can use it the next night.

Another G-MA trick that is a lifesaver! As mentioned earlier (see page 39), hello dough boy (smiles)! Doing this gives me peace of mind. This is a much better alternative for a baby that loves to be warm than a blanket in the crib or a heater in the room, plus I can sleep at night not having to worry.

I simply use a long-sleeve body suit with the blanket sleeper because Madison gets very hot when she sleeps. It works great!

ON THE GO

Put the blanket to cover the car seat under the handle but over the canopy. It is much easier to carry this way.

This may seem obvious, but at first I was putting the blanket over the handle, and it was so hard to get a good grip. I finally saw another mom with the blanket under the handle. I was like, duh!

I actually learned this one from Rachel once Tyler was already a few months old. So, I guess it is not so obvious, Rachel.

Put the pre-measured formula in a clean bottle and carry a water bottle in the diaper bag – this makes the time to make a bottle about five seconds.

 This is a lifesaver at a restaurant! Or on a road trip! Or anytime your baby is screaming for a bottle when you are in public (smiles).

Once again, the 8 oz. water bottles make this even easier! Plus, they are more convenient to fit in the diaper bag!

If you need more than one bottle on an outing, buy a formula dispenser. You can pre-measure formula into three sections and then pack it in the diaper bag. Makes it easy to make a bottle on the go!

When your baby gets older you can fill one section with cereal! I actually have this, and since I breastfeed, I use two compartments for her baby oatmeal (to mix on the go) and the third for cereal puffs.

Also works to sit on the nightstand for middle of the night feedings (anything to help in the middle of the night, right?).

If you think you will need three outfits for baby in the diaper bag for an outing – take four! You will never regret having extra changes of clothes (and if you have friends with a baby your baby's age, you might just be their lifesaver)!

This might be an exaggeration, but, you get the point. Babies always need more than we think they will, especially when we think they won't. Expect the unexpected!

HA-HA! Or you may end up with a boy dressed in his little brothers high-water pants that are bright blue, because his mom didn't pack enough changes of clothes and had to borrow some from little brother...no names or anything (smiles).

If you think you will need six diapers for baby in the diaper bag for an outing – take ten! You will never regret having extra diapers with you. It's much cheaper than having to buy some when you are out!

 And make sure to check your wipe supply before you leave, too. I have forgotten more than once, and it is not fun to be stuck in the bathroom changing a diaper and be out of wipes! It also helps to separate the wipes individually before you put them in the wipes case.

Again, expect the unexpected! Even when you think you know what to expect from your baby's past behavior, it will change…at the least opportune time…guaranteed.

And if your diaper bag isn't big enough for all of these supplies, keep an extra bag in the car full of extra diapers, wipes and clothes.

Sneak one of your own t-shirts in the bottom of your baby's diaper bag. Inevitably you will need it one of these times!

Or, use it as an excuse to buy a new one! Hopefully you will be at a place where they sell them when they are open.

As Nicole mentioned (see page 92), if your diaper bag is not very big, you should keep an extra shirt for yourself in the car, as well as the extra diaper-changing supplies. That way you will still have it if you need it.

Babies love things that light up. Find a baby toy to take with you that lights up, even if she can't hold it yet.

I got a Baby Einstein ™ mp3 player. Watching the lights will make Madison stop crying in almost every situation.

Or in this day and age of the smart phone, get some cool baby apps. Fisher Price ™ has some great ones for little babies. And they even sell a case for your smart phone that your baby can hold as soon as he begins to grasp things.

BONUS
TRICKS

Use the stern NO the very first time your baby touches something. Once a baby starts exploring, she is testing her boundaries, and you are the boundary maker.

With my five children, I never had to move all of my "untouchables" by doing this. However, always move anything dangerous out of baby's reach – better safe than sorry.

Thanks to the advice from my mom on this one, I started it right away with Treydon. It worked like a charm! We would even receive compliments at doctors' waiting rooms about how impressed they were that he listened so well when we told him "NO" as he was approaching the television.

Madison just started reaching for things, but you can bet I will be doing this!

The use of the word "no" at a young age is debatable by some early childhood development experts. They claim it can introduce negativity and damage self-esteem. My belief is that if it is used sparingly and consistently, it does neither of these things.

Starting at a very young age, every time you put the pacifier in your baby's mouth, grab your baby's hand and move it with yours. Before you know it, he will be putting the pacifier back in on his own.

I did this with Madison. She first started putting her pacifier in on her own on and off at six weeks old! It got more consistent with every passing day. It makes car rides much more enjoyable.

I did not do this with either of my boys, and eventually Tyler just gave up putting it in and now he won't even take a pacifier. Which to some parents is a good thing, but in the middle of the night, it is a very bad thing (smiles).

Distraction is your best friend. When your baby starts freaking out, distract her with clapping, a toy, or a change of scenery. She might just forget why she was crying in the first place.

Clapping works the best for Madison. She is mesmerized by watching my hands. Another good distraction is putting your lips on the palm of her hand and humming.

I have a go-to song with Tyler, "3 Monkies Swinging from the Tree". No matter what is going on or where we are, the second I start to sing that song, he stops crying and starts laughing. This also works great as your baby gets older to have him stay still while changing his diaper.

To keep your baby's ears clean, use a bulb syringe to squirt water in her ear, two times each side, at every bath.

 Madison always had a lot of wax build up until I started doing this. It is pediatrician approved, too.

 Learned this by writing this book together!! Thanks, Rachel!

 It's good for mommies, too!

To encourage your baby's verbal skills, mimic his sounds back to him. It also entertains him and shows him what his mouth looks like when he is making those sounds.

 Madison loves it when I do this with her. It has become a game for us.

Who cares if you look really silly while doing it?

This is one of the best things you can do to engage with your infant and build her self-esteem while encouraging verbal interaction!

From the very beginning, clap for your baby anytime they do something new. This not only builds self-confidence, but down the road it makes it easy to teach him right from wrong.

I do this with Madison, and sometimes I get so excited I scare her and she starts crying, poor girl.

I started this with Treydon when he was a baby and it has made my life with a toddler a breeze. I would clap for him for every little thing, from rolling over, to pulling himself up, to eating baby food for the first time. Now, as a toddler, potty training only took two days!

Disinfect your baby's stuffed animals by putting them in the freezer overnight.

This works so good! They stay nice and fluffy while they get clean!

That is an awesome idea! I'm going to go gather some stuffed animals right now.

I recently read that if you put stinky tennis shoes in a zipper plastic bag and then place them in the freezer for 24 hours, it will kill the bacteria and the shoes won't stink. If this works for nasty ol' shoes, imagine what it can do for little stuffed animals!

TWINS

Always take help with anything that is offered: meals, laundry, holding, rocking, feeding, etc... Not a good time to be too proud for help.

This is a good tip for all new mommies. Keep in mind that between 3 to 6 months postpartum, you will have things in a nice rhythm and need less help. But until then, keep a list of items you need from the store, chores that need to be done, or errands that need to be run, so if someone asks, "Do you need anything?" then you are prepared! A gracious smile and thank you is all they need in return. People love to help. Especially people who love you. You are not indebted to them because they helped you, and one day, you will be able to pay it forward.

Plus, it will be nice to get a break from the chores so you can enjoy your baby!

If your twins are difficult to tell apart, paint the thumb and big toenails with a light-colored nail polish. This way if someone changes her clothing, you won't get confused as to who is who!

I was the one who got to have my nails painted! "N"icole equals "N"ails. So you also have to name one of your twins a name that starts with the letter "N". Ha-ha!

I learned recently that someone makes baby-safe nail polish. Lots of fun to be had here.

Oh yes, I love the baby-safe nail polish! So much fun!

Get your twins on the same schedule as soon as possible. If one baby wakes up to eat, wake the other one up. If one baby falls asleep, encourage the other one to sleep.

In all fairness, this requires a team of two to make this happen. If both babies are bottle-fed then each person can take a baby, and diaper and feed her before putting her to bed. If the babies are breastfeeding, the partner can diaper and hold one baby while the other baby is getting fed. Be patient, something really shifts at about six months where schedules kind of click for babies and parents.

I don't know how parents of twins do it! You have my complete and utter respect and admiration!

Thanks, but if you had twins, you would do it, and do it very well!

While breastfeeding is optimum, breastfeeding twins is literally a full-time job. If you are able to do it, wonderful! If you aren't, don't feel guilty about it. Consider alternating your babies during feedings. While you are breastfeeding one, you can hold the other between your legs and feed her a bottle. The next feeding, switch it around. Both babies get mommy time and the health benefits of breast milk.

Mom, you are very talented! Don't feel bad if you can't breastfeed and bottle feed your babies at the same time. I don't think I could do that. But I LOVE the idea of alternating the feedings!

I know some mothers of twins can breastfeed both babies at the same time. Personally, it was too much for me, but if a mom of twins can do it, more power to her!

In pictures it is often difficult to tell which twin is which when going back through them. Until you are able to tell the twins apart in pictures, always pose the twins with the same twin on the right in the picture, and the other always on the left.

I think I was the one always on the right. "R" for "R"achel, right?

Yes! This was a lifesaver, to always be able to tell who was who in photos. It was nearly impossible to tell you two apart when you were very young, especially in pictures.

To encourage individuality in your twins, do not refer to them as the "twins," and correct others if they do. Either use their names, or refer to them as the "girls," "boys," "babies," or "kids." They will thank you later.

 Yes they will! Thank you, Mom!

 THANK YOU!

 See? That was completely unsolicited.

Jennifer with Rachel and Nicole as babies
("R"achel is on the "R"ight)

FOR THE MOM

You will still be wearing maternity clothes for several weeks/months after baby arrives.

 I think I packed mine up at four months. And it sure felt good!

I was still wearing a pair of mine when Tyler was nine months old! Ha-ha!

Don't go jean shopping six weeks postpartum. Seriously.

I did that, and I don't know what I was thinking. I tried on literally 20 pairs, and left the store with nothing but tears. I was so anxious to get out of my maternity pants, but they fit better than anything I tried on! I tried again a month later and had much better luck!

I didn't go until about a year postpartum, too depressing. Maternity jeans are fine, nobody can tell anyway.

Nine months up, nine months down. It took you nine months to put on the weight, give yourself nine months to take it off before thinking twice about it.

OR LONGER!! I am at nine months right now, and I still have ten more pounds to lose until my pre-pregnancy weight.

This is easier said than done, but seriously, give yourself some slack. You have grown a human being, for goodness sake!

For some of us it takes 16+ years to lose the weight. Oh, wait. We are talking about postpartum weight loss? Disregard.

Postpartum bleeding lasts a lot longer than you would expect, usually about six weeks, but then will start and stop randomly for another month or so.

I was very surprised by this. I thought something was wrong with me, but nope!

Always check with your doctor if you are concerned, though.

If you are ever at a point of being very frustrated with your crying baby, it is much better to put her down somewhere safe and leave the room than it is to potentially hurt her due to your frustration.

 YES! YES! YES! A safe crib or pack 'n play is a great place to put your baby while you take ten minutes and regain composure. If you need more time than that, don't let your pride stand in your way. Call someone you trust and ask them to come over and help you. We are all in this together and we need each other. You would help out a friend if she called, wouldn't you?

And don't even feel guilty for it. Everyone needs a break from a screaming baby.

Everyone!

Do your research, listen to all the well-meaning advice from friends, read baby-tip books (smiles), but always, ALWAYS, trust your mother's intuition.

 SO TRUE!! Mother's intuition is a very powerful thing.

Yes, and you always have veto power over anything anyone suggests or recommends!

Even doctors. Talk to them. Tell them your concern. This is your baby, and you are responsible for everything. If your intuition goes against what the doctor recommends, discuss it with the doctor. If you are still not satisfied, seek a second opinion from another doctor.

When you have your first newborn, you will be worried about Every. Little. Thing. That is normal. Don't be embarrassed.

If you want to take your baby to the Emergency Room for one cough in the middle of the night because you are afraid she is choking to death (I might have done that), then DO IT! Even if your baby is just fine by the time you get there (my baby might have been) it DOESN'T MATTER. Your peace of mind is also very good for your baby. And the hospital staff has seen it all before and will be very kind (like they would have been if I had *actually* done it).

By the time your second comes around, you still worry about Every. Little. Thing.

I am lucky I have my mom or sister to call, so I never have to worry very long!

Look on the positive side. For example, when your baby wakes you up every two hours, remind yourself that at least she is still alive.

It really does help. It's hard to stay frustrated if you think of it that way. Side note: when I first wrote this, every two hours was the worst nights I had. Nowadays, I am grateful to get a two-hour stretch! So, remember, it could be worse!

This is much easier said than done, especially in the moment. But always remember what incredible joy your little one brings you and try to make it through one minute at a time. It will soon pass.

A baby has a way of changing your life. Your experience will not be exactly like anyone else's, but some things are common. Feelings of fatigue, sadness, frustration, depression and having the blues are normal. This does not mean you don't love your baby and are not happy he is here. Talking to someone helps. If you have these feelings for two weeks, talk to your doctor. You don't have to suffer. It's not good for you, or your baby.

 Remember that the doctor has seen it all before. She might have even experienced it herself. You are not alone and you don't have to suffer.

Consider joining a new mom's support group or play group. These can be found in your local community or church, or even online.

Don't underestimate the value of connection. We all need each other and to know we are not alone in our joys, struggles, and challenges. Plus, it can be a lot of fun to meet new people who have kids the same ages as yours!

Or ask around to other moms that you know, they may be part of a mom's group already. You can even start your own!

Keep a list of chores that needs to be done, or shopping items you need. When people ask, "Is there anything I can do?", graciously say, "Oh yes! Thank you! I have a list I am trying to get to; does any of it look appealing to you?" People love to help, but never really know how.

Or just give the list to your husband...ha-ha, like that ever worked for me!

People really will want to help you any way that they can. Just say "thanks" and let them.

When family comes over to see the baby, especially in the first few months, make sure you are not cooking and cleaning for them while they are holding your little one.

This can be a complex one to navigate. Maybe you can simply show them this book, and ask them if they wouldn't mind helping out with the tasks so you can relax and hold your baby. I don't know, Rachel, Nicole, do you have anything here? It's such an important one.

I'm not good at cooking or cleaning without a newborn, so I'm not much help. But I will say, the newborn snuggles go by much too quickly, and the last thing you want is to look back and have regrets about not holding your baby enough.

Yes, and if you are missing your baby when the family is visiting, simply tell them that. They will be more than happy to give you your baby back.

Cousins!

FOR THE
WORKING
MOM

Time does not stand still. Savor **EVERY MOMENT** you get to spend at home with your little one before you have to return to work. Don't try to be super mom. Sitting at home all day simply holding your baby is great, because once you go back to work, you will never have that chance.

 This was really hard for me to learn. It is so hard to actually savor the time you get to hold and snuggle your little one without thinking about the million other things you have to do. But FORCE yourself to stop and enjoy those moments. Before you know it you will have a toddler bouncing around all day. The last thing you want is regret.

The times that are the most meaningful for bonding with your baby are the transition times: waking up routines, bath time, and bedtime. If you are at home during these times, embrace them. It will go a long way in you and your child's relationship.

I always make it a point, no matter how hard of a day I had at work, or how willing my husband is to help, to put my boys down to bed. Many days I leave the house long before they wake up, so our "bonding" time is bedtime.

Nicole does a great job at this. No matter what, she is there for these moments with her boys!

If you need childcare, and can afford it, it is worth the little bit of extra money to pay someone to come to your house to watch your baby.

I have done both ways, and it is so much less stressful having someone come to your home, in your surroundings, to watch your baby. Plus, this way you don't have to worry about interrupting your little one's sleep schedule. Taking my boy somewhere else, I would spend thirty minutes every night gathering all the supplies he "might" need the next day; precious time I could spend cuddling my baby if I had someone coming to my house.

Maybe you have a family member that is out of work that would be willing to do it for you.

When you think you don't have time to enjoy your kids that is the exact moment you should stop whatever you are doing and go play with them. Play and laughter make life so much happier than a clean kitchen.

 It took me too long and too many lost moments to learn this.

This is very true. You can also strap on a baby carrier while you do your housework. Then you get time with your baby and the housework gets done.

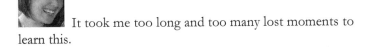

To save time: when folding laundry, just put your baby's clothes in piles of what they are, i.e.: shirts, pants, pajamas. Baby clothes don't wrinkle, and you can spend more time playing with your little one.

So true! The small amounts of time saved from minimizing daily tasks can really add up to extra bonding time with the kiddos.

I started doing this after my second was born, and it really does save me so much time. And all working moms know, time is a very valuable thing!

You can even just pull clothes out of the dryer until it is time to do laundry again.

If you have to travel, video chat is a lifesaver. You can see your little one and he can hear your voice.

Or even on a lunch break during a long day at work! We do that with my husband. It makes his day just a little bit better, and Madison loves seeing her daddy!

This makes the time apart not nearly as hard. I'm so grateful to be a working mother in this day and age with all of this wonderful technology!

When you leave for work, if your little one is awake, always say goodbye to him and tell him you are going to work (don't try to sneak out the door). This will help so he does not feel abandoned. This also helps reduce separation anxiety if you do it from a young age.

I did this since my first boy was about four months old, and at almost three he has never thrown a fit or tantrum when I have to go to work. He just gets that it is part of life, and knows that I will be home soon to play with him.

Great advice! And yes, Treydon is amazing with his acceptance of going to work being a part of life.

FOR THE DAD

Since we aren't dads, and never have been or ever will be dads, we got input from our husbands on tricks for dads.

Spend your free time for the first few months cooking and cleaning so the mommy of your cutie can spend her time snuggling and bonding with your new little bundle of joy!

OKAY-- just kidding. I wrote that one! In a dream world I would love to do nothing but snuggle and cuddle with my newborn. Those days go by too fast! Just reminiscing about it makes me want to go snuggle a newborn!

Ha-ha, so funny, Nicole! But feel free to show this to your husband and tell him we said so (smiles).

Take any chance you can get to bond with your newborn.

My husband says, "The first few months are hard to get quality time with your baby because he is breastfeeding so frequently. You can feel like you do not have much to offer. My favorite thing to do was to sleep with little Treydon on my chest during his naps. I felt so close to him. This was our time and looking back, it is something I will never forget."

YES! Trey loved to snuggle with Daddy because of his strong arms and chest; he was much more comfy than Mommy was.

My husband says, "My favorite memory with Madison is those first two days at the hospital when Rachel was still a little out of it from her C-section. I got to spend all night with Madison in my arms. Those are the moments you never forget."

Keep a burp rag in your back pocket.

My husband says, "Looking back at pictures of when Trey was a baby, I looked like a mess. My shirt was always covered in spit up, but I was just so used to it, it didn't even phase me. With Tyler, I kept a burp rag in my pocket, and now looking at pictures, I would actually frame them (smiles)."

HA-HA! We did have so many cute pictures with Trey and Dad that never made the frames because Dad looked like he hadn't done laundry in weeks.

I actually put a receiving blanket through my belt loop, leaving one end at the perfect length to reach Madison's face while I am holding her. That would work for dads, too.

Cleaning and scrubbing can wait 'til tomorrow.

For babies grow up, we've learned to our sorrow.

So go away cobwebs, dust go to sleep.

I'm rocking my baby and babies don't keep."

Author Unknown

Tyler, Treydon, and Madison in October, 2011

Do you want to learn even more great tricks and tips to help you as your baby grows?

Using your smart phone, scan this QR code to go directly to the 3MomsTips Facebook Fan Page!

Or you can visit us at:

Facebook.com/3MomsTips

Twitter @3MomsTips

Please email any comments, suggestions, or your own tips to 3MomsTips@gmail.com

12007619R00074